IN CELEBRATION OF

_____

GUESTS

NAME	NOTE

GUESTS

NAME   NOTE

GUESTS

NAME	NOTE

GUESTS

NAME   NOTE

GUESTS

NAME	NOTE

GUESTS

NAME   NOTE

GUESTS

NAME	NOTE

GUESTS

NAME   NOTE

GUESTS

NAME	NOTE

GUESTS

NAME	NOTE

GUESTS

NAME	NOTE

GUESTS

NAME	NOTE

GUESTS

NAME	NOTE

GUESTS

NAME   NOTE

GUESTS

NAME	NOTE

GUESTS

NAME

NOTE

GUESTS

NAME	NOTE

GUESTS

NAME	NOTE

GUESTS

NAME	NOTE

GUESTS

NAME

N⊙TE

GUESTS

NAME	NOTE

GUESTS

NAME	NOTE

GUESTS

NAME	NOTE

GUESTS

NAME

NOTE

GUESTS

NAME	NOTE

GUESTS

NAME	NOTE

GUESTS

NAME	NOTE

GUESTS

NAME   NOTE

GUESTS

NAME	NOTE

GUESTS

NAME

NOTE

GUESTS

NAME	NOTE

GUESTS

NAME   NOTE

GUESTS

NAME	NOTE

GUESTS

NAME   NOTE

GUESTS

NAME	NOTE

GUESTS

NAME

NOTE

GUESTS

NAME	NOTE

GUESTS

NAME

NOTE

GUESTS

NAME	NOTE

GUESTS

NAME   NOTE

GUESTS

NAME   NOTE

GUESTS

NAME	NOTE

GUESTS

NAME	NOTE

GUESTS

NAME	NOTE

GUESTS

NAME   NOTE

GUESTS

NAME

NOTE

GUESTS

NAME	NOTE

GUESTS

NAME

NOTE

GUESTS

NAME	NOTE

GUESTS

NAME   NOTE

GUESTS

NAME   NOTE

GUESTS

NAME	NOTE

GUESTS

NAME

NOTE

GUESTS

NAME

NOTE

GUESTS

NAME	NOTE

GUESTS

NAME	NOTE

GUESTS

NAME	NOTE

GUESTS

NAME	NOTE

GUESTS

NAME	NOTE

GUESTS

NAME   NOTE

GUESTS

NAME   NOTE

GUESTS

NAME   NOTE

GUESTS

NAME	NOTE

GUESTS

NAME

NOTE

GUESTS

NAME	NOTE

GUESTS

NAME   NOTE

GUESTS

NAME   NOTE

GUESTS

NAME   NOTE

GUESTS

NAME	NOTE

GUESTS

NAME

NOTE

GUESTS

NAME   **NOTE**

GUESTS

NAME   NOTE

GUESTS

NAME	NOTE

GUESTS

NAME	NOTE

GUESTS

NAME	NOTE

GUESTS

NAME	NOTE

GUESTS

NAME	NOTE

GUESTS

NAME   NOTE

GUESTS

NAME	NOTE

GUESTS

NAME   NOTE

GUESTS

NAME	NOTE

GUESTS

NAME

NOTE

GUESTS

NAME   NOTE

GUESTS

NAME	NOTE

GUESTS

NAME

N⊙TE

GUESTS

NAME

NOTE

GUESTS

NAME

NOTE

GUESTS

NAME   NOTE

GUESTS

NAME   NOTE

GUESTS

NAME   NOTE

GUESTS

NAME   NOTE

GUESTS

NAME   ## NOTE

GUESTS

NAME	NOTE

GUESTS

NAME

NOTE

GUESTS

NAME	NOTE

GUESTS

NAME   NOTE

GUESTS

NAME   NOTE

GUESTS

NAME	NOTE

GUESTS

NAME	NOTE

Made in the USA
Monee, IL
07 June 2021